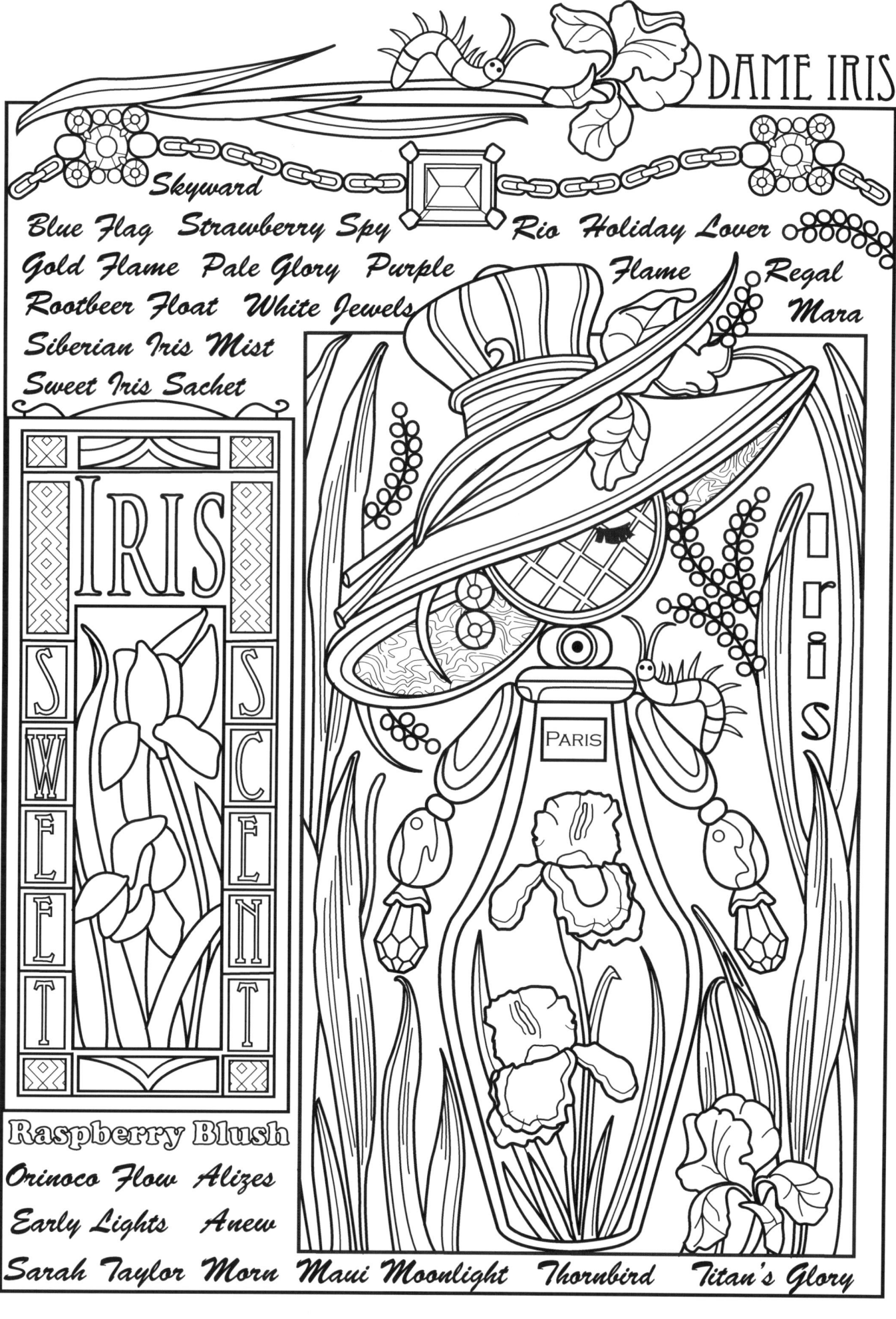

LILY OF THE VALLEY

Coty Muguet des Bois   En Passant
Diorissima April's Kiss   Fair
Our Lady's Tears   Joy

Penhaligon

May Bells

Parfum

Lily of the Valley signifies "the Return of Happiness"

Freesia

South African plant

LEMONY FREESIA

ZESTING

Freesia symbolizes innocence & friendship.

Lady Primrose

Tryst
Primaverde
Moon Safari
Tendre est la Nuit

L'Amour Cologne

Take a stroll down the Primrose Path...

Thank you for choosing this coloring book!

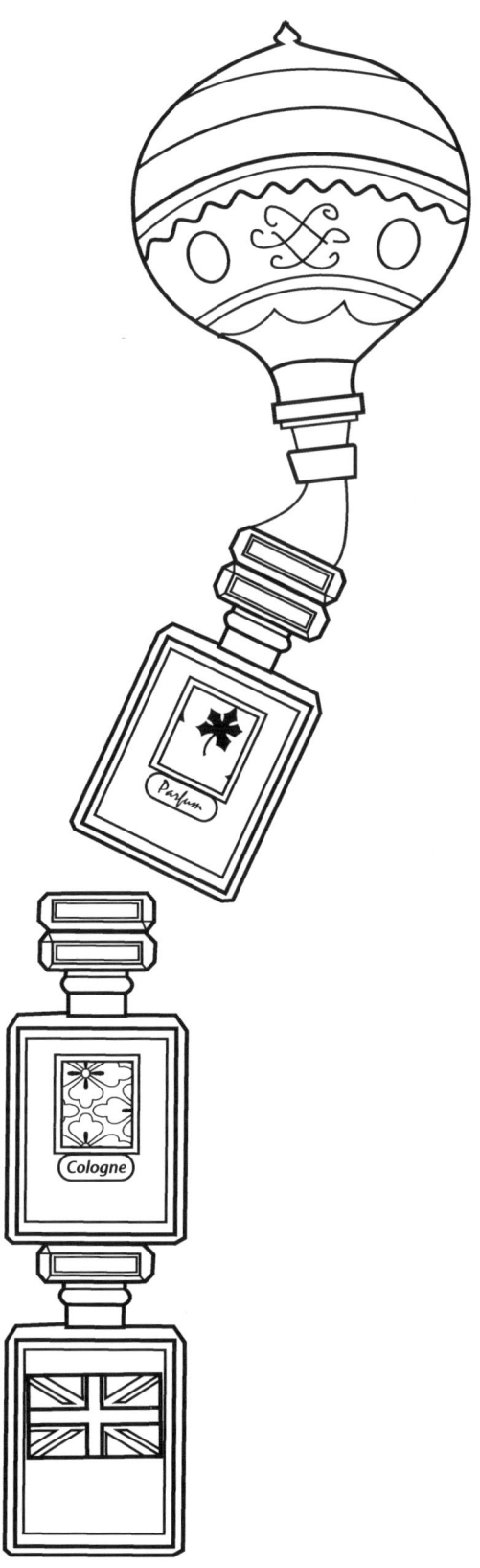

Made in the USA
Lexington, KY
19 March 2019